I0186529

IT ONLY HAPPENED ONCE

JANE YELLOW

JOZEF SYNDICATE

JANE YELLOW

It Only Happened Once
Text and cover design copyright © 2014 by Jane Yellow
Cover design by BJ Graphics www.bjgraphicsonline.com
Published in the United States by the Jozef Syndicate
ww.jozefsyndicate.com

All copyrights reserved. No portion of this book can be reprinted without the
written consent from the publisher. For all permissions, write to the Jozef
Syndicate, Post Office Box 40864, Baton Rouge, LA 70835, (225) 925-5693.
For author interviews and speaking invitations, email projects@jozefpa.com.
Events, locales, and conversations have been recreated from the memory of the
author. In order to maintain anonymity in some instances, names of individuals
and places have been changed, including some identifying characteristics and
details such as physical properties, occupations, and places of residence.

LCCN:

ISBN-13: 978-0615955698
ISBN-10: 061595569X

Printed in the United States of America

January 2014

ACKNOWLEGEMENTS

Special thanks to everyone who helps and supports me: my family, ex-coworkers, and Christian brothers and sisters, who prayed for me and helped my family. Thanks to all of you. I thank God for the love of family and friends. Thanks to my husband, my sister, my church family, to a special aunt, my mom, and my dad. May God bless you all!

INTRODUCTION

ABUSE OF ANY NATURE IS WRONG, WHETHER verbal, mental, or physical. It's wrong! This book is the story I've lived and I thank God for the opportunity to share how God has brought me through so much pain and suffering. It is my prayer that someone will be delivered from domestic abuse as a result of this book.

The abuse I suffered at the hand of my ex-husband only happened once and as a result it almost cost me my life. But God had other plans and they were for my good. Jeremiah 29:11 states, "For I know the thoughts and plans that I have for you,' says the Lord, 'thoughts and plans for welfare and peace and not for evil, to give you hope in your final outcome.' "

My inspiration to write this was given from above to heal, to revive, to comfort, and to strengthen. *It Only Happened Once* is my story to share with the world. It's a story about the very thin line that separates love from hate and how quickly a person can become abusive and violent. It's a story about losing love, losing children, and losing friends at the hand of one act of escalated domestic violence. It is also a story of how God's most amazing love can surface out of the most horrendous act of physical abuse and attempted murder.

Thank God for a winning outcome!

Table of Contents

LOVING MY MEN

EVERYWHERE WE WENT, JAMAR YELLOW WAS taking pictures. Ready or not, he'd snap that Polaroid instamatic like a professional. As an attractive 35-year-old Louisiana "Redbone", I had absolutely no problem smiling for his camera. And, no one had problems smiling for Jamar, who's 6'3" frame was wrapped in muscle and the smoothest brown skin a girl could imagine. I don't think he even had two percent fat in his whole body. He was outgoing, loved working out, playing sports, and bar-b-queing. White girls were even crazy about him. There were a lot of eyes on him and on me but never once were we jealous. We were an outgoing, fun-loving couple and so in love. I was enjoying life with him and my teenage son, Quinton. Quinton was my 15-year-old son and my heart. We grew up together. I loved him so much. He was respectful and very protective of me.

The three of us would shoot basketball, go swimming, play dominoes, and hang out with friends, always laughing and having a great time. We weren't much on drinking or smoking heavily.

I had been in law enforcement working with legislators when my son was in middle school. There wasn't much I would back down from in those days. My friends saw me as fun, dependable, and outgoing. (I thought I was average; they thought I was smart). I had been divorced for ten years and dated off and on with nothing serious. When my cousin introduced me to Jamar after church services, he and I clicked.

Jamar was a well-rounded person. We liked many of the same things—including dancing. He was a gifted brakesman and truly enjoyed his work. I was a security officer, and we both worked long shift hours. It seemed as if ladies had great crushes on him all the time. There were a lot of eyes on me with a lot of questions because I was the first Black female hired for the position at my new job.

I would complete new self-defense classes to learn new techniques for the job and would stay up at night practicing what I learned and doing rounds of crunches and pushups to be stronger than a potential attacker. I'd try to get Quinton to be my practice buddy. Although he could easily carry me over his shoulder, he couldn't handle my strength.

I remember times I'd bounce around the house like I was Ali or Frazer, saying, "Come on, Quinton. Come get your momma." He'd say, "No, no, Mamma. I don't want to wrestle with you. You're too strong." I'd follow him around with my little bounce, tapping his shoulder, trying to edge him on so I could get experience with a real person. "Nah, Ma. I'm serious. Get away." Then he crawled under the dining room table and I would laugh and laugh. I'd catch Jamar and tussle around with him and without fail the fun ended with him complaining that I was strong as an ox. I was strong, lean, and weighed 135 pounds. He and Quinton became friends quickly.

For the two years that we dated and throughout our brief marriage, Jamar and I would take romantic walks in the park and go to Baskin and Robbins for ice cream every Sunday. Every other weekend, when I was off, we would go shopping for clothes. Jamar would say, "Let me see that on you." If he liked the outfit on me and I didn't, I'd tell him, "If you like it, you wear it." We'd laugh and would leave it right there. Jamar had great taste in clothes. We shopped for everything from church clothes to lingerie. Those were good times. If I worked, he'd shop by himself, always buying something for me. He liked for me to dress up for him to take pictures. On the way out the door to church on Sundays, he'd take pictures of me.

We were churchgoers. We gave offering and tithed after every paycheck. I loved singing in the choir. I'd been a church girl, singing since I was twelve years old. If I missed church because of work, Jamar would be there and tell me the sermon as if he was recording it just for me. There were times—about three times—we tried to go out on a date to night clubs. We soon decided it wasn't a fit for us. So, we started taking rides through Baton Rouge, St. Francisville, and down country roads, talking and laughing in the car like teenagers. At the spur of the moment, we'd go riding. We kept a blanket in the car and on pretty days, we would stop at the store to get ingredients for sandwiches and have an impromptu picnic. Quinton, who was with us most of the time, would say, "Uhh, ya'll need to quit."

We had a beautiful relationship, filled with love. At first it was a long-distance relationship because his job required traveling away from me for extended periods of time. The last year of our dating, our relationship really flourished. We felt we no longer wanted to be apart so we decided to live together until we got married. We both worked locally during the days and we were able to come home each day.

We married August 1989 and in October, I was blessed with a security job at a local plant with great benefits and the money was good. We started preparing for our future and decided we would move out of the apartment we were in and into a nice three bedroom, two bathroom duplex until we had enough money saved to purchase a home together. Things looked promising for us.

I was where any young woman wanted to be. I felt like I was on Cloud 999—not just Cloud 9! I had never seen my son so happy. My son would say having Jamar in his life was like having a big brother and a stepdad in one. "I can tell him stuff and we wouldn't have to tell you, Ma," Quinton would tease me. "We tight, we hang out." We were an outgoing, fun-loving couple and so in love. I was enjoying life with Jamar and Quinton.

Jamar was never the type of man to hit on a woman. He spent all his time being affectionate towards me. He seemed to live for affection and intimacy. Jamar would say, "You're not with me a lot so when you are here, I'm going to shower you with love." And he really did.

Knowing I was getting married and getting ready to start a new job was happening almost too close together—I was just amazed. I mentioned to Jamar that we should revamp the wedding and maybe push it back a while. But I remembered him becoming upset, saying he feared he'd lose me. He knew I would be working with and around a predominantly male environment and maybe that concerned him. He questioned how could I love him so much and have second thoughts about marrying him.

He said if you love me we'll get married as planned. And I quickly let it go. I had the man I wanted.

Had I had a personal relationship with God, instead of just attending church, I do believe I would have gone into prayer and realized that I had not heard from God in reference to marrying Jamar. I saw what I wanted him to be. Because he'd be the first to get to church, was a dedicated worker and a faithful family man who professed to love the Lord, I just knew in my heart I wanted to marry this man. I felt he truly loved and adored me. The time he spent talking to my son, hanging out playing basketball with him and even swimming together, made them thick as thieves. Quinton looked up to him with respect as his stepfather. They went to ball games and movies while I was at work.

Jamar worked straight day shift with every weekend off. This allowed him to have one on one time with my son. This put the frosting on the cake. I told myself Jamar was the one I had been waiting for. But truthfully, I had not heard from God Almighty and I didn't even realize that I should have gone to God about Jamar.

IT ONLY HAPPENED ONCE   13

The first time I saw Jamar truly upset about something was about eight months into the marriage. He was so upset that he cursed. I was totally shocked. For years, this man had never cursed or showed any serious anger. This particular time, he was mad that the plant where I worked had not hired him. He was moody the entire day. It was like he needed to let go of something that he hadn't let go of. In the back of my mind, I now wonder if he was jealous that I was making more money than he was, especially since I'd gotten the job.

On Christmas Eve of 1989, I was in a dangerous situation at work where I could have died. My co-workers later remembered Jamar being in the room the night of the situation. Family members were looking for relatives and asking questions, while the conversation of compensation for death was being discussed. A contract worker remembered Jamar asking how much money the families were going to get for the employees who may have died. He was told $500,000, if the employee died accidently. We had talked previously about the benefits of my job which included a life insurance policy of $250,000.

I recalled how upset my son was that Jamar wasn't the least bit upset that he could have lost me. He said "Daddy Jamar, you not mad something almost happened to momma."

"Aww, man. Your momma's alright," Jamar said.

Quinton mentioned it a second time to my mother. "Daddy Jamar didn't seem too concerned when we couldn't find momma."

She said, "Baby, We all were worried about Jane. Don't think that way."

There were no red flags or warning signs that led me to understand how that incident and the information about my benefits would give Jamar about eight months to plan and get the courage to kill me.

IT ONLY HAPPENED ONCE   15

A DAY I'LL NEVER FORGET

IT WAS SUNDAY, AUGUST 5, 1990, A DAY I'LL NEVER forget. I had completed a 12-hour work shift at the plant and I was anxious to get home and spend the afternoon with my favorite men: my new husband and my boy, Quinton. I pulled up to my residence to go inside and the car door lock jammed on me. It was some kind of malfunctioning. I couldn't get out of the car. After several attempts, I was able to unlock and open the car door. Jamar met me at the door with a very long passionate kiss. I told him what happened with me trying to get out of the car and he replied, "Oh, it's probably something simple. I'll check it out." He then proceeded to tell me that he had made arrangements for Quinton to spend the night at a friend's house so we could have quality time to ourselves because he had planned a night of passion.

He relished on how he had missed me so much due to all the overtime I had been working. And, besides, our first anniversary was coming up. As we moved to the master bedroom, he said, "I bought you some new bubble bath, Sweetheart." Of course, this was not unusual. He would always shower me with candy, perfume, flowers, and any goodies he thought that would put a sparkle in my eyes and a thump in my heart. He even ran the bath water that night as he did on several occasions. He said he was getting it all prepared for the big night of passion. "This will be a night of passion you will never forget, Baby," he kept saying. What woman wouldn't want that? He would sit on the toilet while I bathed and just listen to me go on and on about work or friends. We would talk about our future.

This night was no different.

After drying off and sliding on my nightgown, I went to the far right side of the bed. He was in such a hurry for this night to continue. I told him my toenails were in much need of a trimming because they were making holes in my socks. "And I don't want to cut you with these," I said, anticipating this passion-filled night Jamar kept promising.

I sat on my side of the bed next to a window, clipping my toes, as he sat on the opposite side of the bed watching a taped football game. The room was small enough that he could sit on the bed and change channels to the television within two or three steps of the bed and dresser. I was trying to hurry up for this night of passion planned on my behalf. About the time I started to cut the fourth nail on my right foot, Jamar rose up. I didn't give it a second thought.

All of a sudden, he grabbed me around the neck and picked me up, holding me up with his hands, choking my neck and definitely not in a loving way. His hands were squeezing his fingers around my neck in quick motions. I was unable to scream as I was kicking my legs trying to free myself from the grip but to no avail. He had the tightest choke on me and I couldn't do anything about it. As I struggled, wiggled, and kicked he chocked me harder and harder throwing me to the bed. He grabbed my neck again and started punching me with his fist in my face as hard as he could. Ok, this was not passion. *What happened? Who is this hitting me?* I couldn't breathe. I thought my head was going to bust. I even thought maybe I could knee him in his groan since he had straddled me, but I just couldn't move him. He was entirely too strong! Unnaturally strong! He was definitely not the man I married. Finally, after what seemed like an hour of him punching me, he rose up, and I somehow was able to roll off the bed to the floor and started crawling. I couldn't stand up. Blood streamed from my face. The pain was unbearable. I couldn't catch my breath but I had to get away. I then crawled between the nightstand and the headboard, but he grabbed me by the feet and pulled me out to the open floor area. I still tried to crawl away—anywhere—even up the wall. But everything was slippery with my blood all over it.

He walked around the bed, grabbed me, and drug my body away from the wall and the bed. I was weak. I couldn't think of where I had put my gun.

He grabbed the 19-inch television that was plugged next to me and started slamming it down on my head. As if that wasn't enough, he stood on top of my body and busted the flesh from my body with the television slamming it forcefully. How many times? I don't really know. I couldn't move nor scream! I was losing a lot of blood and was whipped in and out of consciousness. "Oh, you gone die tonight, B&*ch!" he yelled. "You gone die! I'mma get this money." I remember even holding my breath to make him think that I was dead. That I was gone. But my body flinched! He yelled, "Oh you're not dead! You're going to die tonight!" I heard the TV crash, broken on top of me and I felt a sharp shock. He continued beating me, trying to kill me. He jumped up and down on my chest and stomach over and over again crushing bones and driving pain through my body to the floor. I couldn't see clearly. Everything was blurred and, in my weakness, I couldn't stay fully awake.

The home phone rang. I could hear him talking but I was completely paralyzed. At a glimpse, I could see him walking past me. I must have passed out! I had to have passed out! For how long? I don't know. I just know I was laying on the floor and just thinking maybe it's a bad, bad dream. But it just couldn't be because I was hurting all over. I had difficulty picking up my head. I had a faint voice. But inwardly I cried out, "Lord, help me! Don't let me die like this!" I knew I was hurt pretty bad because I couldn't hear my own voice.

Then, there was a dim light and somebody was moving my body. Who was it and where were they taking me? Someone carried me out the room, through the hall, and to the front door. I remember the door was already opened. It was like I was moving on air. I wasn't aware I was seeing out of one eye. The other had been dislodged out of my head and was resting on face which was swelling quickly. As I was carried out, my feet weren't touching the floor. I was floating. I was so near death, I couldn't have walked if I wanted to; my body was too weak—too broken.

I was carried out of my home. It was nighttime and the streets were quiet. I was propped up against a few feet away at the door of my cousin's duplex. Her door opened for me. I was placed on my feet to stand but I was so weak I stumbled into her home. My feet were making baby steps, pain shot through my body. My head felt like it was exploding. I held onto the furniture and wall of her hall as

I struggled to get to her bedroom door. I still couldn't scream but I saw her son come out of the hall bathroom. He looked at me and screamed with so much fear, "Momma! Momma!" She opened her bedroom door and I fell right into her arms. I heard my cousin scream, "Oh my God! Jane, what happened? What happened?"

I whispered with everything, "Jamar." I desired to live and not die! They had to know who had beaten me so brutally. I had no idea that I was so disfigured. I looked in humane.

Angel screamed for someone to call 911. She told her husband to get towels. I heard her say my head had been busted open and that I had a mouth full of glass and my tongue was hanging out. She screamed, "Get help! What's taking so long?" I could barely see but I could hear people talking saying, "Hold on, Jane. You're going to make it. You're going to live! You can't die!" I heard hollering, "More towels! More towels! The bleeding is bad!"

"I'm going to get her to the hospital. They're taking too long," Angel said.

"Lady, don't move her!" I didn't recognize the voice.

"It's the fireman!"

22   IT ONLY HAPPENED ONCE

"Wait, put this c-collar on her neck. Looks like it might be broken."

Then I heard a loud siren and people yelling, "Over here! Over here! Hurry up! I was trying to talk probably to the paramedics. I was trying to describe the car Jamar was driving. All of a sudden a voice said, "Don't let her talk. She has only one side of a face." I'm sure I was in and out of consciousness.

Before the paramedics could take me away, Angel's son had begun calling family members. I remember being afraid of what they would do him when they found him. Tempers were really flaring and family members were ready to see blood. They were mad, enraged, bitter and very dangerous.

My throat was closing up. I was in excruciating pain. My head was huge. I was holding on for my life.

TRAUMA

I LAID ON THE GURNEY IN THE BATON ROUGE General Hospital's trauma ward. I was shivering in pain. I couldn't lift my head or see well enough to make out faces. The sounds floating through my ears brought in pain on both sides of my face. I was in and out of consciousness and everyone was moving so quickly to save me. While the doctors were working on me I could tell they were dumbfounded. "We're going to have to just try to stabilize her first," one doctor said.

I could feel the movement of people around me but they appeared like hazes of colored silhouettes. My face was so distorted and broken that my head had expanded almost four times its human size. There were tubes coming out me in all kinds of ways. An opened c-cord braced my neck and the doctors were re-placing the eye into its sock as delicately as they could to save the eye.

My nose was completely flat. The right side of my face was severely broken. My mouth was busted and swollen badly. My teeth were knocked out of my gums. They struggled to sedate me fearing I would have a heart attack. I had a ruptured ear drum that kept me from hearing everything that was being said.

"Does anyone know what happened?"

"There's some kind of glass in her face."

"Ma'am can you hear me?"

The machines were beeping. Their feet were scraping the ground. It all hurt my ears.

"Here's some morphine, Doctor."

"Put it in now. Let's keep her alive."

I could see the light from the hall as the door opened. But, I couldn't move my head. "My God! My God! No. No! That's not her. Noooo!" It was a woman's voice. She was crying so loud. Two women were standing

IT ONLY HAPPENED ONCE   25

together holding each other. The taller one was my adult daughter; the short one who touched my hand was my aunt. They'd come to identify me. "That's her. Look at her hands and her rings." They were thanked and quickly pulled out the room into the hall. By then a Baton Rouge police officer had been stationed by the door and my identity changed with the hospital records in order to protect me.

The next thing I remembered was someone saying to get in touch with my mom. I don't know when or how soon my mother came, but through very blurred vision I saw my mom's face.

When the detectives came to get my statement, I was able to tell them one-word answers, "Yes," I am Jane Dolly Yellow. "Jamar" had attacked me. "Yes," he did all this by himself; "No," we were not fighting. "No," he had no weapons that I knew of. "No," he is not injured. "Yes," that's the car and license plate number. "No," he wasn't drunk or on drugs, and "No," I don't know where he may have gone.

The damage to my body consisted of all these things and much, much more: Collapsed lung, ruptured ear drum, cracked skull, broken nose, collapsed sinuses, bones broken on the right side of my face, right eye knocked out, teeth knocked out of the gums, bruise on my brain, some of the nerves in my face was severed, damage to my bladder, and tissue damage around the right eye. To this day, I have no feeling in areas of the right side of my face and the right side of my lip.

I can no longer drink from a can for fear of cutting my lip. There's no vision in my right eye. I have silicone tubes in my nose that runs to the corner of my right eye. I have vocal cord damage. The pallet under my tongue was torn loose.

The fine bone was removed from my head and the flimsy thin skin was removed from around my brain that allowed the doctors to rebuild the right side of my face and to frame it. To rebuild around the right eye, the thin skin was use to close the big hole because of the damage to my septum. However, there wasn't enough skin available so I live today with a large hole behind my septum. All but three teeth that were knocked out were put back in the gums. Also screws were placed in the bones of my gums and my mouth was wired shut for what seemed to be at least two months or more. Traction was applied to align the face and pull it over from the right side to the left.

To close my face, it took 187 clamps and more than 200 clamps to close my head.

I remember the doctor telling my mom that he was not sure that I would be able to see out of my right eye. She insisted that they re-socket it and allow me to keep my own eyeball. He then said, "If she lives, she would probably be a vegetable and never able to work again." My mom was in disbelief and she sat their quietly.

While I was still in critical condition, the human resource officer from my job came in at my request to change my beneficiary benefits. We quickly changed it from Jamar to my mother in the event that I didn't make it. It is truly a miracle that I am able to perform the way that I do now.

During the time my mouth was wired I ate from a straw and communicated with paper and pencil. After six weeks, the doctors went back in my head to retrieve more bone because in order to reconstruct my face. After three months, I would return to work because I needed sixty days to make one year service which would allow me to keep my medical benefits. There wasn't much I could do except sit in a chair. After a couple of months, I was in the hospital again. This reconstruction went into twenty or more surgeries, and I constantly had to go back for more and more reconstruction. My nose was rebuilt which took several surgeries. Screws have been placed in the bones in my mouth to stabilize the teeth and they remain there to this day. There were surgeries to rebuild my eye and the partition under my tongue.

When the bandages were removed from having the right eye re-socket, I had to have multiple surgeries to reconstruct my face around the eye. I finally got to see my face. Through a wired mouth I screamed! The face in the mirror had no features that looked like me. I looked like an animal with parts of a human face.

I was swollen, my head and neck were huge, my eye was swollen shut, and my mouth was hanging on the right. (I looked like that poor boy Emmett Till who'd been lynched in 1955. His mom showed the world her son's beaten, swollen body on the covers of *Jet* magazine to put the brutality on display. Just as I am showing you mine on this book's cover). My head was four times its normal size. The nurses couldn't move my body because my head was so swollen. It took nearly two months for the swelling to be manageable. Looking in that mirror, I saw how Jamar had crushed my face. The right side had totally shifted! I cried out, "Oh my God!" I was shaking, crying, "Is this me?!"

My mother responded, "That's you, baby. It's not as bad as it looks."

Hurt, disappointed, disgusted and in disbelief, I said, "Lord, You kept me here, You didn't let me die. You have got to fix me. Fix me so I can live in Your world. Don't let me look like this. Fix me, Jesus!"

I don't remember Quinton seeing me in the trauma ward but I knew he was aware of my state and he was angry. I was just blessed that he did not find me on the floor bleeding to death. I am grateful for that hand and those arms that carried me into my cousin's house. My boy would not have survived finding me dead. I thank God for that.

The third surgery lasted nine hours. After having been placed in the intensive care unit at the hospital, a nurse was stealing the morphine that was to be given to me for pain. Still unable to talk, I was able to write and let the doctor and my mom know about this unthinkable attack. My mother was absolutely furious and threatened the nurse with bodily harm. She said, "My baby is fighting for her life and you are trying to kill her. Woman, I will break your neck!" Soon after, the doctor and my mom agreed it would be in my best interest and wellbeing to be moved to another hospital. I was then moved and thank God I did not have that problem anymore.

This abuse only happened one time in my three-year relationship and marriage to Jamar and that one time almost ended my life.

My aunt saved a clipping of a newspaper article about the attack. What was printed was no justice to me. It was very upsetting to read the description of the attack as a domestic dispute—which was the first lie. The story was written as if the abuser just hit me three or four times and that it was over. Lie number two, in actuality, he hit me more than two dozen times, slamming the 19-inch television down on my face and head. I was hit so many times my head was burst wide open. They didn't report that my face had been torn open and flattened because the bones were severely broken and that there was flesh missing from my body. None of that was reported.

One of my family members who truly love me was so angry and furious with my attacker that he hired a hit man to kill Jamar. He tried to bail Jamar out of jail with a brief case containing twenty-five thousand dollars in cash to bond Jamar out of prison and have him killed.

While news about that was coming to me in the hospital, someone should have been trying to get me an attorney because a trial was inevitable. What public defender would look beyond this being a Black-on-Black crime or look beyond the news report that lied and stated that the attack was a domestic fight? Who would really see me as a real victim and not "another dumb woman in a bad situation"? I needed my own attorney. My family was so focused on either revenge or getting me strong enough to leave the hospital that no one thought about the attorney.

On a weekly basis, my supervisor from the plant would visit me in the hospital. He would have money and a page of signatures. Co-workers from each department and every shift would wish me a speedy recovery or let me know they were praying for me. I'd be amazed when he would stand there and count out the money. It was always at least a thousand dollars. "I know it's not much, Jane, but we want to help you make it through this," he would say. I heard him tell my mother on one occasion that if we couldn't get anyone to help me at home that he and his wife would take me in and care for me.

Make no mistake God will supply what you need. I thank God for the doctors who had a spiritual bedside manner. I thank God that they believed in prayer and asked God for knowledge and wisdom to perform the necessary surgeries on me.

When my mouth was unwired and I stopped eating through a straw, it was painful to chew because the bones in the right side of my face were shattered from being broken so badly. Even though the fine bone from my head was used to rebuild my face; it was still difficult to chew. It took time to eat even small amounts. I had to chew slowing and carefully. Partial plates with plenty of wires were made to help frame my face and slowly but surely I started chewing better over the years. Even today I have to be very careful of how I chew or I could unknowingly bite the side of my mouth and cause it to bleed. There are places on the right side of my face that still have no feeling. I will never be able to drink from a can for fear of cutting the right side of my mouth. I wouldn't know it was cut until I tasted or saw blood. It's hard to fathom someone plotting to kill you when they were so nice to you. I question myself over and over and over again as to why didn't I see some warning with Jamar. I still have no answer. But I'm so grateful to God for where I am today. I tell you, I am truly blessed to be here.

As a cosmetologist, I was able to place hair extensions in my hair without people really noticing where the bone was removed from my head. I also perfected my makeup to cover the wounds and sagging on my face. Using makeup techniques and a thin layer that looks like skin, I can hide the worse of my facial wounds.

The internal wounds still remain but the mercy of God and the comfort of the Holy Spirit has truly become my covering.

STRENGTH TO OVERCOME
GOD SUPPLIES WHAT WE NEED

Through all the pain and suffering, I stayed in prayer. I found myself talking to the Lord all through the day and night. He promises if you just call on Him and believe that He's able, He will answer. I had to pull back and draw on everything I'd learned about God since I was a child. I had to remember God is not a man that should lie, neither the son of man that He'll have to repent. But if He said it, in His word, then that's enough. His word is a lamp unto my feet and light unto my pathway. God would never leave me nor forsake me. I was not alone. He's a good God! I took in scripture constantly and believed earnestly in Psalms 30:5, Psalms 23, Psalms 27, Psalms 90, and Isaiah 54:17. I was not about to give in; I hadn't any other time in my life and I wasn't about to now. Through the Word, I gained strength, power, and courage to make it through every minute, hour, day, night, month, and years—up until this moment: twenty four years later. I made it!

THE TRIAL

JAMAR ENTERED THE COURTROOM UNSHACKLED and un-handcuffed. He walked in looking like he was already the champion. He strolled in his prison uniform, head high as if to say "I am the Great Jamar, ain't nothing going to happen to me." I had so much medication in me; I was so mad I was seeing blood. If I could have reached him, I would have killed him with my bare hands.

Without my own attorney, I had to sit in the audience as the case of the State of Louisiana vs. Jamar Yellow began. Very little was said about me. In fact, I can't recall them even mentioning my name nor the details of the attack. They didn't mention how after the attack he had pushed his vehicle into LSU lakes and gotten in the trunk to fake his own kidnapping. The lake was too shallow that the car got stuck instead of continuing into the water. When officers found him, he told them, "Help! Help! I've been kidnapped and they killed my wife!" according to law enforcement. None of that was presented.

They only shared the fact that Jamar had not had a previous record and this assault was his first. I would have killed him if he opened his mouth. He never said a word in court. It was pretty much in and out the court within a matter of hours. I felt the outcome would have been different had my family members focused on getting an attorney for me instead of concentrating on revenge. I wasn't looking for money. It was a fair judgment and punishment that I was looking for from the court. I could not get to an attorney for myself and relied on my family.

After the case was presented, I was called into the hallway for the attorneys to tell me the judge had offered Jamar a plea bargain. I was devastated! Because he had no prior records the prosecutors felt he would get less time. I broke down. I couldn't believe what I was hearing. After speaking with the prosecutors and going back to the courtroom, the judge sentenced him on the spot to ten years. It made no sense to me, but years later I remembered that Jamar's mom knew a lot of judges who she had done domestic work for over many years. Maybe that had contributed to him getting a light sentence. There had to be a reason why the system was failing me. (I had not realized then that the justice system had failed countless women and victims of violence.)

Jamar's sentence started with credit for time already served under the Good Time Sentence. I didn't know then that he would stay in jail only a few months shy of five years in prison. Then, he walked away a free man.

His mother became enraged after hearing her son's ten-year sentence. She screamed to the judge, "Don't give my son that much time! She still has one eye to see out of!" Even though my mouth was wired, my hands weren't cuffed. I wanted to strangle her. Friends and family had to restrain me from getting to her. As I looked at my son, his face was covered with rage and revenge. As Jamar's mom left the courtroom, Quinton was right behind her. I feared what was going through his mind and what he might do to her. I had to get to him. We caught up with them in the elevator. Before I knew it, Quinton had grabbed her and held her eye-to-eye with him. "What did you say?" he asked her.

We all went into a frenzy trying to calm him down.

"Not now, Q."

"Don't hurt her."

"Don't be like him."

"She's going to get what she deserve, Q."

"Let her go, God's got her baby, please."

Although we all felt the emotions that Quinton had, we had to prevent him from doing something that he just might regret. When the elevator doors opened, we pushed Quinton out of there as fast as we could. I held him with all my might. I needed my boy. A few of my cousins stayed in the elevator to talk with Mrs. Yellow. At that point, I didn't care if they were nice about it or not. I wanted her and Jamar out of my life forever.

After going to jail Jamar would constantly write letter and even call home saying he was sorry and that he loved me. I had to contact an attorney to have the correspondence from him stopped. In a rage, I put a handful of letters in the barbecue pit and burned them. He had some nerves to write and call me. I wanted nothing, nothing at all to do with that one. I was left with a life time of memories and pain.

I later found out that one of my fellow co-workers arranged to have Jamar beaten and raped frequently while in prison. In all honesty, that wasn't satisfaction for me. I didn't care about him losing his manhood I wanted him locked up for life. But once again the system is not set up for the victim. He was serving a very short period of time for attempted manslaughter instead of life for attempted first degree murder which he deserved. I had a life sentence. He deserved more.

FRIENDS

MY BEST FRIEND OF EIGHT YEARS, MISSY, MUST have visited the hospital while I was sedated, though I have no recollection. With my mouth wired I could not call her but I'd ask about her on paper almost every day. When I'd been released from the hospital under the care of my aunt, she finally called to see how I was doing and said she would come over with juice. I would look for her and just listen for that door bell to ring, wanting so badly for her to hold me in her arms, to comfort me, and to tell me that she loved me, but it didn't happen. I waited and waited. Late that afternoon, she called and asked my Aunt Tee to speak with me.

"I know you been waiting for me," she said.

My mouth was wired shut and I could only moan out, "Um-humm."

"But I gotta be honest with you. I'm not coming."

I was silent.

"Girl, people wouldn't beat a snake the way he beat you."

I was still silent.

"I have a problem with looking at you the way that you look."

That hurt me so badly. I was able to blurt out a muffled, "Then, don't look at me!" I was so distraught over that, so, I just hung up the phone and to this day I have not talked with her. That let me know then that she wasn't a true friend even though we were always together, shopping, cooking, and doing typical things friends do.

Even my pastor had a problem seeing me how I was. He said, "This can't be her," until he remembered my hair was a honey blonde color. "This must be her," he said. He had married us and thought, like everyone else, that we were a great couple. He had even spoke nicely of Jamar and how great it was for me to have such a good husband.

42   IT ONLY HAPPENED ONCE

After seeing me in the hospital, his thoughts of Jamar changed. "Jamar really fooled me," he said. "But, that's what the devil's like: wolf in sheep's clothing."

When I made it to church, the pastor took liberty to speak his mind from the pulpit in the presence of the entire church. He went into detail telling the congregation how swollen my head was. I wanted to go under the pew. Everyone was looking at me. He told them the details about my facial features and said I looked like an animal. I had to resist the urge to stand up and yell "shut up!" My cousin, Angel, told me, "Put your collection in and keep walking." As I look back, I can't imagine what he was trying to do by telling the congregation in that manner. I haven't figured it out. I never went back.

Seems like all my friends deserted me at a time that they should have really been there for me. I made myself sick many days by needing to have my friends in my life, but that didn't happen. Even today, those friends remain my ex-friends. I knew abuse could tear apart friendships but I could not understand how this one time incident that was so brutal would cause me to lose the people I felt were my lifeline.

I realized God was all I had. I continued to ask God to give me a miracle healing to fix my face and my heart. I knew then that it would not be easy being disfigured. I was desperate to fit in, even though at that time I was confined to the house for another three months. Since, I had declined home health assistance, my aunt moved into my home to care for me. We returned to the home where I almost died.

She took me to the doctor weekly and sometimes twice a week. I was always afraid of what the doctor would do as he worked to pull my face back together. After every visit I would be in excruciating pain. I don't know how I had the strength to bare it.

In the waiting room and anytime I was out in public, I would have my head down or cover it with a towel or anything that would hide my face. "Don't worry about them," my aunt would say. "You're still here. They're going to fix it, baby. It will be alright."

I would think of my old friends and sadness would try to swallow me in when my aunt would comfort me saying, "Baby, we love you. We accept you any way we can have you because you are beautiful to us."

She was lying.

My face was messed up!

I was messed up!

My eye was messed up!

My mouth was wired!

My head was busted open!

She just lied.

But at the time, I sure did need to hear that lie over and over again. Besides, when I was sick I told people I was wonderful. It was what I needed to do for me.

I was still in a sort of dazed state; I didn't want to accept how bad things were for me. I wanted this to be a dream. Her little lie was the little push I needed to get me closer towards strength. *One day, what she was saying would be true; but today it isn't.* I told myself. It was comforting because the majority of the time I was in pain and I would keep it to myself.

I had no friends and in this condition I wasn't making new friends. Although, I had returned to work. I was focused, isolated, and terrified of the lingering eyes and unasked questions. I had gotten help in the hospital from a national foundation that awarded me a small grant to pay for living expenses. (Today, there are plenty of resources and help available that I was unaware of then and many did not exist at the time.) I reached out to two domestic violence support agencies for help. A coworker told me the local agency probably would not help me because of my race. I just knew she was wrong.

When I called the local battered women's agency, sure enough they asked my race. I told them, "I beg your pardon? If I am an abused woman and I'm looking for help, why would my race be a factor? Don't even worry about it!" and slammed the phone.

I'd even gotten up the courage to talk with a counselor at my company's employee health program. A few days after our supposedly confidential session, she and another employee passed my security booth. She said to other woman, "She's the one I was telling you about." The other woman looked at me like I was some new attraction at the zoo. I told her, "If you want to keep your job, you'd better not let me hear you discussing my personal business with anyone ever again." That was truly devastating. It was bad enough that where my job was the people could see me as they entered but at least I couldn't hear them saying anything. It was also bad that Jamar's photograph was posted at every entrance to the property as a dangerous person.

I felt like doors of comfort were being closed in my face. Even though I was fearful, scared, and paranoid, I decided to get help a different way. I knew The One I could go to and I wouldn't have to hear it again. So I allowed this to push me closer to God. I knew He would keep me. After having had those incidents, I became withdrawn and stopped seeking help.

I was a member at a small church and a couple of the deaconesses visited me but there were no real support groups for people who had gone through the stuff I went through.

Nobody from my church was familiar with resources to get help. None of that type of support happened for me. It was like I was in another world. That's why I had to pray so hard to keep my sanity. I prayed, *God hold my mind. Keep me. Clear my thoughts. Fix me, Lord!* God showed me He was a friend that truly was closer than any sister, brother, or friend. I knew that God was and is everything I need. So, I continued to exist from day to day, still living in fear but I kept the faith and prayed and I was determined to go on with my life. I just couldn't and I wouldn't give up living.

Yes, I started blaming myself. I would say to myself *I should have felt something. I should have seen some kind of a sign that they all would leave me.* But how could I when Jamar, Missy, and my other friends professed to really love me.

DAYS WHEN

THERE WERE TIMES WHEN I LAID IN MY BED, plotting in my mind how I would slowly kill Jamar if I ever had the chance. I wanted him to suffer for what he had done to me. I had been nothing but good to him. I thought about shooting him in both legs and stabbing him so he couldn't get to me. I thought even about boiling water and pouring it on him as he would try to crawl away like I had tried. I wanted to burst his head open and let his brain be exposed like he had done me. I thought about just shooting him in the face, then the arms, and watching him slowly die from the lost of blood. Even as I drove down the street I would look for Jamar. After my family took the guns I had for protection, I felt very unsafe. I decided to buy another gun and I did it through a fellow coworker who ordered guns for others in my department. I planned in my mind if and when I would see Jamar I would shoot him or even run over him. I had plans to empty the pistol on him and make certain he was completely dead. The rage and vengeance crept inside of me with so much power, it even scared me. Fear drove me straight to God because this was not God's plan for me to carry such devious thoughts out. I prayed to God to remove the hatred from my heart. Instead of plotting it out and executing it, I turned to God and was delivered from the evil thoughts. As I reached out to God, I asked for forgiveness.

I made no drastic changes in my life. I prayed for discernment to know when I heard from God. I actually heard voices speaking to me. I was being told, "It's well; God's got it." I knew that was the Holy Spirit ministering to me because I'd read that God would never leave nor forsake me. I could hear the voice of the Holy Spirit inside of me. I knew it was His because it completely contrasts my own voice or the devil's voice running through my mind. The distinction is that the Holy Spirit's voice is only about good. Prayer coupled with the word of God helped me to know what to do. I realized that if I would listen, the Holy Spirit would minister to me. So I spent a lot of recovery days praying and listening to the Spirit of God.

God truly made a difference in my walk, my talk, and my thoughts. It took some time for all the thoughts to leave me but I stayed focused on my healing. Instead of thinking about killing, I prayed about living. After being delivered from the hate in my heart I was able to see much, much clearer. And I gave a good look at my life.

I stopped loving Jamar the day he tried to kill me. My Aunt Tee was telling me, "Sometimes you have to try to work things out." I told her, "I almost lost my life, not my damn mind! There was no way in hell I would work things out. As soon as I could I would get rid of this last name!" I knew then it was time for her to go and time for me to get around on my own. Everything been replaced. I had gotten rid of it all room by room from silverware to furniture and photos, over my own time little by little. I didn't want the memory of Jamar nor our life together.

I struggled to release myself from guilt and shame. *This wasn't my fault!* Getting past how I looked was hard. I didn't want anyone looking at me. I didn't want to look at myself. If there were any signs of what Jamar was planning to do I certainly wasn't aware.

I remember when I first started driving myself around. When I would go to a store, I'd go in and out as quickly as possible. If I saw someone who I knew, I would go up another isle to avoid them. Shame will drive you plum out of your mind. It was hard to be productive when I was operating in that state of mind. I would stay inside because I dreaded seeing people who I knew. All I could imagine was their eyes fixed on me and how I looked. It was hard enough having to look at myself let alone having eyes piercing me through and through. I stayed hiding from people and holding my head down when I would pass someone, as if I did not see them. This made me feel ungrateful. There I was repenting and telling God thank you for saving my life but I was exhibiting shame.

I never thought I'd not have sight in one of my eyes. I was half blind trying to do everything that my two eyes had done in the past.

To be somewhere and know what you are capable of doing and not be able to do it was hard. Even being at home after work or on my off days was hard. To leave my apartment, I would peek to see if anyone was watching. And if the coast was clear, I would sit down on the steps and slide down the flight of stairs on my behind and hands dressed for work. Can you imagine how embarrassing?

I left home almost two hours before my shift at work begun so I could avoid the headlights of vehicles as much as possible. Because of the nerve damage, the oncoming headlights would make my right eye water and that affected my good eye. It's hard driving when you feel tears running in your nose and your mouth and not on your face. I was driving with my feet and knees shaking because, with only one functioning eye, I could barely see. It was a struggle driving with a rapid heartbeat constantly calling on the Lord. One 15-minute drive took me 45 minutes. Sometimes it would take me an hour or longer to take the 15-minute ride to work.

Just going to work and coming home was hard enough. All I could do was lay down in bed, try to make it to the next day, and try to deal with a problem teenager. I was quickly losing my son to his own anger.

Depression fell on me like an anvil. I really felt like a zombie. I felt like I was drowning in awful pain and hurt. I was drowning in this physical storm. I was totally paranoid. I snatched down the pictures of Jamar around my job. I'd gotten to the point where I just couldn't continue seeing images of him.

The doctors had me on medication that kept me partially sedated where half the time, I didn't know if I was going or coming. I was functioning at work like a zombie—medicated and still working. I wasn't totally aware of what was going on and I was so glad they had lightened my duties substantially. I was—and still am—grateful. I knew it was important that people saw me on the job, working. Besides, I needed it for the medical benefits so I worked as hard as I could to perform like I had prior to the attack.

After several surgeries, I returned to work with very limited functioning and worked until the next scheduled surgery. In and out, in and out but, God blessed me to return each and every time. It was so hard as I heard people talking and saw people starring.

The trauma I'd experience haunted me daily. I was so fearful that as I would be driving I would hear Jamar's voice coming from the back seat of the car. I would hear him telling me to pull over to the gas station so he could purchase Kool cigarettes. There were times when I was so paranoid that I prayed to God to just keep my mind because I felt like I was really losing it. It became worse as I could see his face in other people and I would have to immediately go and pray.

The hallucinations turned into nightmares but I was so determined to learn to live with what had happened to me. I would have such terrible nightmares and wake up crying, "Lord, I need you!"

I could actually feel God's presence. Even on those nights I ran into the closet for safety. I remembered being wrapped in clothing as if I was covering my body to protect it, and in actuality I was in a dream state running from Jamar. I would wake up on the closet floor and peak under the door to make sure I was still alone and I was safe. That day I wouldn't be able to go to work even if I tried. I had to call in sick. I was worn. I was shaken. I was weak. I needed comfort.

I pulled out a list of scriptures on healing and protection (Psalms 91) that the mother of my former church shared with me after her fight with cancer, and I would cling to them. I particularly liked Isaiah 54:17, "No weapon formed against you shall prosper, And every tongue which rises against you in judgment You shall condemn. This is the heritage of the servants of the Lord." I'd read that because I was always afraid that Jamar would get out and come back and get me. That he would come through the door at any time or climb through the window.

Whatever room I was in, a Bible was there with me. Those scriptures helped me to start my day. I read them over and over throughout the day, every second that I needed to feel comfort until I became strong enough to go on. All I could do was pray a day at a time just to survive. The Lord became my therapist and my everything through this whole ordeal.

I had to finally admit to myself that this was not a time in my life to be too proud to ask for help. I knew I could not see how to drive so I paid a coworker to transport me to and from the job. I found someone to braid in the blonde-brown hair I needed to cover the gash in my head.

Then, wow!

Things really started looking up after several months. I was fitted with eye glasses to help my left eye and I started driving again. I did this always with caution and hardly driving at night. I took back my large car and bought a smaller car and this helped me with judging distance when turning and parking. For the longest time, I would have to park the car, get out and look at the lines, and get back in the car to park correctly. There were just so many challenges and so many medical obstacles from that one night of abuse.

I remember a time when I was praying to God to remove fear and anxiety I was having about an upcoming surgery. I knew until I completed the surgeries I wasn't going to get to the recovery I needed.

One day, I'd driven myself to the cleaners. While I was in line, someone touched me on my shoulder to tell me a lady outside sitting in her car was beckoning for me. I went to the door to get a look at who it was, and I couldn't quite get the glare out of my eye. She waved for me to come to her.

"I don't know who that is," I said.

"Come here, baby, I'm not going to hurt you," she said. Although I was functioning in total fear and depression every day, there was something about her that made me feel it was okay to talk to her. The sun, which was behind her, casted light around her almost like a halo. I was forcing my eye to focus so I could see her. She was radiant and in a glow. She was so beautiful. Her hair was so beautiful it looked like it had been colored onto her head.

"Yes ma'am," I said.

"Don't be afraid, baby, I have message for you," she said, still sitting in her car. "You are about to have surgery and God said to tell you it's going to be okay. He had taken you through the other surgeries, and He wouldn't leave you now," she said.

I was shocked. I didn't even know her. She had to have known something or I wasn't talking to a regular person. I thought she must have been a prophetess.

"Let me touch your hand. I'm not going to hurt you." I touched her hand very quickly. "You are a blessed child." She touched me and I quickly pulled my hand back when I felt hers. Other than that I would have thought I was hallucinating. I walked carefully back into the cleaners, trying to look back at her out of my good eye. I didn't want to fall or draw attention to myself. When I got back in the line, I looked out the window to see her again and she and the car were gone. Disappeared. Just like that. I said, "Where she went?" No one in the line responded. I couldn't wait to get home.

I called my grandmother hollering and screaming like somebody crazy. I told her what happened.

"Momma always told you, you better be careful how you treat people because you might be entertaining angels," she said. "You have so many angels they are all around you. When you need them, they show up. Sweetie, you were just entertained by an angel"

I said "God what am I supposed to do now?"

God was all I had. I depended on God for everything and he was everything I needed.

I wanted to look better but I'm tired of the cutting on me. I would be so afraid. I would pray, "Just don't leave me, Lord. Bring me back in my right mind. Make sure you wake me up," I would pray. Nurses asked what really happen and they would kneel on the side of my bed and cry like a baby.

However, I stayed in prayer. I read the Bible daily and it made me stronger.

As I read the Bible, I began to stand on God's word. The battle wasn't mine, it was The Lord's! So I turned it over to The Lord because I had no way of working out anything in my life. After praying and praying and praying I stood and waited and waited and waited and waited. It was in God's own time the healing manifestation started taking place in my heart, my mind, and in my body. But God was not through with me yet. A lot more healing needed to take place in my life.

Even now there are days when my right eye is irritated and it runs, affecting the vision in the good eye. There are days when scarred tissue and mucus harden and get trapped in the hole behind my septum. There are days when I have problems with my throat and I can hardly swallow. I have severe headaches and days when my mouth hurts. There are days when I could just take my right eyeball out and free myself of the pain. Because Jamar crushed my esophagus, many days and nights it is difficult to just breathe. These days are so numerous.

My doctors just recently had to stretch my esophagus to aid in swallowing. There are nights still (24 years later) when I am so afraid all I can do is cry and pray for God to hold me in his arms. I could feel an embrace. I am soothed and comforted, and I am able to fall asleep.

LOSING QUINTON

AS I SIT HERE AND WRITE THIS BOOK THAT HAS taken me 24 years to write, I feel good about myself. I'm better today! My life is better than ever before. But, I so wish I could say the same for my son, Quinton.

Even though, you hear people talk about children being resilient, as adults we are still able to cope with life situations far better than our children. Quinton's life has never been the same since he was the 15-year-old boy who saw the results of a brutal attack on his mom by a man he adored and respected.

Quinton soon became very angry, bitter, and revengeful all the time. He was very rebellious and stopped listening to me. He constantly said he was responsible and that he should have stayed home that night instead of visiting a friend. He would have protected me, he would say. And, I know he would have. My son would give his life to protect his mom. It hurt him in indescribable ways to look at my disfigured face and to see me in constant pain and agony. He would say, "I swear I'll somehow get in prison and take care of him for sending me off for the night so he could kill my mom!"

My child had no reason to fault himself. I was responsible for him; he wasn't responsible for me. Any mother can look into their child's eyes—especially her son's eyes—and see a pure, deep, unconditional love that nothing could shatter. Quinton had that kind of love for me. He'd call me his Mack Momma and we talked about everything. We were so close and in so many ways, he and I grew up together. While he matured as a young boy, I was maturing as a mother and we helped each other through life especially since I was a single mother. For a decade, it was just him and me. The thought of almost losing me was disastrous to his young mind.

"Momma, whatever the cost, even giving up my freedom, he will pay by my hands for what he's done to you!" Quinton would say.

For a while I could calm him down by telling him two wrongs would not make things right. But then it got to the point where every time he saw me hurting, it would make him more and more enraged. And I was in a constant state of excruciating pain that I couldn't hide it from him. He knew me too well! I pleaded with my child to accept counseling and go to therapy but to no avail. He started cutting classes, skipping school, staying out all night, hanging with the wrong crowd and started using drugs. He was so rebellious, I feared what could happen to him. I constantly told him, "Jamar attacking me was not your fault! It was about collecting my insurance policy! It was not your fault! There is no way you could have known!"

I refused to give up on my son; I had to get him help. I didn't want to lose my baby to the world of crime. I needed him. I didn't want to be alone at home. I was terrified. My travel through the obstacles of recovery kept setting me back and knocking me down, but God kept picking me up. As I continued surgery after surgery, my son got completely out of hand. I prayed to hold on to my mind. He broke the law and served six months in a juvenile detention center. He was so mean that he beat a young man and busted his nose and blackened the young man's eye because he was in a rage of anger. I explained to him he wasn't helping me or himself. He didn't want to talk about God, but I continued to pray for him and tell him about God. He'd been in church since he was a little boy. I taught him about God. I prayed with him and taught him the importance of prayer.

After serving six months in detention, my son was worse and angrier than when he went in. Being locked up was no eye opener for him. He just didn't want to do the right thing. His heart was full of revenge, desperate to hurt anyone—especially Jamar—the way he and I had been hurt. He refused to listen to my parenting. After a short year of freedom, Quinton was arrested again on drug charges. My child lost his freedom. He served thirteen years; after being released, he had problems living in society. He still didn't want to do the right thing as an adult.

It makes me wonder how the children behave with mothers who were in abusive situations far longer that I was. My abuse happened just that one night. There was no build up to that moment. Quinton was not in an environment of fighting, disrespect, or abuse. And that one night completely ruined his future. I do believe God has a plan for him in spite of what has happened, I only wish he had listened as a young boy and released the anger and hurt. I wish I was strong enough then to get him the emotional help he needed to gain closure and move forward. Abuse is traumatic on a child in ways we can never ever know and it is worth the child's life and soul that we remove ourselves from abusive relationships—at all costs.

I miss the relationship that my son and I had. We were very close and I'll never give up on him. I look to God for my strength and there's so many days when I feel so weak and had no way to help Quinton. But God is my present help! As a parent, we truly want the best for our children. He passed up what could have been an excellent football career just to try to get even. Truth is, Quinton never even came in contact with Jamar while being incarcerated. God wouldn't have it happen that way. Vengeance is His, not my son's.

DIVORCING YELLOW

IT WASN'T EVEN THREE MONTHS AFTER THE attack when Jamar begin calling me by telephone at the house. Then the letters begin. I don't know who family members thought he was that they would give me the phone when he called. They should've been asking who the caller was. I thought initially, they must have thought Jamar was Officer Allen, the detective who interviewed me in the hospital. Officer Allen called a few times before to see how I was doing, startled that I was alive and answering the phone. One time he said, "I can't believe you are on the phone seeing the condition you were in. There's no way this is Ms. Jane." (I would see him again in court and he would tell me the same thing: "It's unbelievable that you are talking.")

Maybe they thought, Jamar's voice and Officer Allen's were similar so they gave me the phone. I don't know why, but I immediately knew the calls had to stop. Jamar would call like he was right next door. He would talk about how much he loved me and that he was so sorry he did "that".

"Sorry I hurt you, Bae!" he'd say, "But we are going to work this out."

He thought I would be stupid enough to take him back. In his letters, he would write about getting out and back to our lives, enjoying Baskin and Robbins ice cream as before. I thought he had lost his mind for sure.

After the first time, he called a few weeks later. I'd gotten six or seven letters from him within the first six months of him being incarcerated. In one of them, he wrote "the devil told me if I killed you, I would have enough money to support my habit." I put a handful of letters in the barbeque grill and burned them. I wanted nothing to remind me of Jamar Yellow. I had to contact an attorney to have the correspondence from him stopped. "You've got to stop this fool," I demanded. "He acts like he's coming home from work. Like he can come in my life at any time," I said.

"Did he threaten you in any of these letters?" my attorney asked.

"I don't know! I don't want to hear from him," I said. There were no threats in the letter, but the attorney was able to move quickly and have communication from Jamar stopped. I also filed for a divorce; I absolutely had to get rid of the last name Yellow.

I was already left with a lifetime of memories and pain. By the seventh month, my attorney had had it stop. But, I had to wait for the divorce because Jamar had a right to contest it. He was given the same marital rights as a free man. Due to the nature of the divorce, the judge granted it and allowed me the right to return to using my maiden name.

HAM RADIO AND THE HOLY SPIRIT

IN 1992, MY SOCIAL LIFE BEGAN TO EVOLVE. Although I had shied away from meeting new people, I was still pretty sociable with many of the workers in the plant. There were groups of shift workers who I'd eat with during company lunches and another group I made sure were included in different activities as the others. There were women workers who I could tell were in bad situations and I would make it a point to be friendly to them. Because of my health, my eye, and my fears, much of my relationships were related to work, which is where I met Wesley.

Every now and then Wesley would stop by my post and make small talk until he finally got up the nerve to ask what I did after work. Once he found out I had no outside activities, he began encouraging me to do more things.

"Why you keep bothering me, Wesley?" I would ask him.

"Because I think you are too beautiful to be locked away!" he would answer real quick.

"You don't know anything about me, and I ain't interested!" I told him.

"I know what I need to know," he said.

We became friends and I realized he knew I had been hurt before but didn't know the extent or if it were an on the job accident or something else. And it didn't bother him. "I know you're beautiful inside and that makes you beautiful on the outside to me," he said. Believe me, it was only two years later and I wasn't buying no smooth talk from no man. So Wesley faced a lot of resistance. He was laidback and fun-loving. He introduced me to his friends in ham radio and to his motorcycle club friends and riders from across the nation who accepted me as I was. They showed me an unbelievable love and friendship. These were people from all walks of life. They were educators, doctors, lawyers, and people of all kinds of professions. This motorcycle group's home base was in Pensacola, Florida, and we traveled miles and miles around the country visiting numerous states.

Wesley taught me the ins and outs of ham radio and I learned Morse Code. I had always been a quick learner. When I first applied for the law enforcement job at the plant I scored 98% on the first testing. I had integrated the high school in rural Louisiana, and I was the first black female hired in law enforcement at my job. I was never a bump on the log, and I wasn't about to be.

We would get on that radio and talk to other amateur operators all across the world. It was nothing to connect with someone in Africa or Japan. A few times, Wesley invited me to a sort of ham radio convention at the Great Hall in Baton Rouge where operators gathered and talked for two days to other operators around the world. We even took ham radios into local schools and he and I would reach other schools in another country and let the students talk to one another.

There was more to my life now than pain, surgeries, nightmares, and medication. I started to feel alive again. Wesley took very good care to make sure I was safe when we were on the bike. Even though he did not know the extent of the attack, he knew I was physically fragile. He made sure I was comfortable at campsites. And the women riders were consistent companions. They didn't know me before the attack, and I felt like I was starting over. Yes, I still kept my makeup on and used my hair to cover my head wound, but I did not *have* to hide my face. For a year, I was starting to trust life again and enjoy people.

Then, Jamar resurfaced. He was being paroled.

PAROLE HEARING
I was not notified about the hearing through proper protocol but from an unknown caller on Tuesday, October 19, 1993, who said Jamar was about to get out of prison. The notice went to my supervisor. "Do you know that there is a parole board hearing on Friday for Jamar?" asked my supervisor. I said "no".

That Wednesday, I decided to do some investigating with no help from the District Attorney's office. When I called the parole board office, I was shocked to know that there was a parole hearing and my employer was notified—but not me—that there would be a hearing Friday, October 23.

I started to freak out. There was no way I could live where I was living because he would come back and find me. I was still in the place where I almost died.

I had to act quickly. I called family and the police department to request the crime scene officer's presence at the hearing. I explained not being notified and I really needed them there. The chief of police at the time said that no officer had been requested by victims at parole hearings before but he would grant it and have an officer there.

Upon arrival at the parole board hearing, the police officer who did the crime scene was present. Also present was a van load of supporters that included family members and coworkers. I was totally shocked to be confronted with an all-male panel of parole board officers. I did not seek council and I represented myself. No one else could represent me the way I could. After all, the violent domestic abuse had happened to me.

Jamar had already been given two breaks. He had a chance to plead guilty to man slaughter with ten-year sentence but he should have been tried for attempted first degree murder and a sentence of twenty years. He was instead sentenced under the good time law and took a reduced sentence.

"I do not know how long I would be able to live in this nightmare. I was in constant prayer for my sanity," I told them.

"I've seen people break down like babies crying over this forsaken crime and the pain that they've seen me go through, and today I ask God's mercy at this hearing. I feel it's unfair that such an inhuman, vicious beating inflicted upon me that Jamar would be given only a ten-year sentence and for me, the victim, my sentence is life; I've not even committed a crime."

As I spoke with the parole board members, I pleaded with them and I prayed to God that Jamar would not be set free. I said, "He is dangerous, and he should not have any rights. He disfigured me. He mutilated parts of my face. He is a sick, inhuman, uncaring person. Please do not give him the chance to return to society and possibly kill me. I've suffered enough from the tortuous beating. I plead with you that you reject this inmate's parole."

The pictures I carried were those before any surgeries had been performed. It was not a pleasant sight for anyone to look at. I shared with them the police report where Officer Allen had written that they could see where I literally tried to climb up the wall in my own blood trying to escape. Blood was splattered everywhere. It was not a domestic dispute. It was a vicious, premeditated attack.

Even with the severity of my injuries and Jamar's obvious intent to kill me, the fact that Jamar had no prior criminal history got him a short time in prison. He ws not paroled that time. But Jamar was a free man who served less than five years.

I could only imagine the state I was in when Wesley and I finally spoke. I had taken the doctor's advice to add an antidepressant with my other pain medicines. And one day after he could not reach me by phone, he came over, worried. He found me outside in my robe and nightgown, sitting on the wet grass. He knew something was off and got me to go in the house. I was able to explain that my actions were a result of the medicine and not some major issue I was having. That was the last time I took it. I was not about to give my life away. God had saved me for a reason and it was time I started to understand why He kept me alive.

By now, Wesley and I had been dating for several years. He was my guardian, constantly looking after me. I knew I was safe with him. He even went as far as giving me a motorcycle and purchasing a full-size RV for my comfort at the campsites. Wesley helped me to rebuild my self esteem and start to really live again. He was an asset in my life. He helped me come out of hiding. He said I had a beautiful heart and that made me a beautiful person. The things I learned from him helped me go forward in my life. I was never looked at or treated different than anyone else. I will forever be grateful for his friendship

God used the women at the campsite to truly comfort me, though. I remember being in Reserve, Louisiana, at a site. It was night time and my level of fear had intensified. I was terrified out there and it was unbearable. I couldn't hide it. I just knew Jamar was nearby and he would get me. I believed the women at the site noticed something was wrong but no one said a word.

I had been watching Miracle Parker for a while and I could tell something was truly different about her. Then the Holy Spirit told me to tell her about Jamar and I did. Little did I know that night would be a night of release for me and for a few of the other women gathered there. One of the women must have heard us talking because soon I was telling all five or six of them about that night and how I was slowing coming back together. They cried. Some were crying for me and some were crying for themselves. I knew then that it was time for me to begin helping women.

Miracle, a fearless prayer partner, helped me pray through the new struggles I was facing by opening myself up again and constantly dealing with my lost son. Wow! How God awesomely provides what you need when you need it. Miracle would make it a point to pray with me and check on me regularly. The Holy Spirit would always let her know when I had the urge to just give up and she'd come through like a tornado with prayers to rescue me.

She prayed with me and I grew closer and closer to God. I began to have a personal relationship with God that was constantly growing. I even began to hear His voice more clearly for myself and he was telling me to move on from Wesley.

Holy Spirit
Are you serious?! I would ask God internally. *It's time to end this with Wesley? Why now? That must be a mistake.* I was in a tug-of-war with the Holy Spirit constantly nudging me to end the relationship. I couldn't understand why. Wesley had reconnected me to life again. I had friends because of his influence. I had a new little hobby in ham radio and was enjoying seeing the country. Yes, I was occasionally smoking marijuana or drinking alcohol to kinda fit in but it wasn't in excess. And yes Wesley and I were sexually active and not married. But, he loved me and I was growing to love him. *Why would it be time to stop now?*

I didn't know the answer but I did know that I wasn't about to move forward in anything else without God.

So I begin to step back and watch Wesley through the eyes of someone who wanted to please God and I starting seeing things about him that I really didn't like. At first I thought they were minor things but, remember, once God told me to get out I begin looking for reasons why I should get out. And God showed me. Although Wesley truly cared for me, our lifestyle was too reckless and I longed for something more than the next motorcycle ride. So, I stopped riding.

I also stopped riding motorcycles because of fear. There were several riders who lost their lives because of the way they rode the bikes. This was very painful to me because of our relationship. They were my new extended family. Some even received injuries that caused medical problems for the rest of their lives.

One incident in particular was when I lost two friends at the same time due to a motorcycle accident. This zapped my urge to ride again. I feared I would get injured and would never heal. With all the things that had already happened to me with my near death experience it was truly time to hang up my chaps and so I did. My mom even hated the fact that I was on a bike riding up and down the highway on two wheels. If she knew I would occasionally drink and ride, she would have had a hissy fit. That was her way of saying," I hate that you've gone through so much and now you're riding a motorcycle."

I honestly hated Jamar for the brutal beating. I hated the pain and suffering I endured. At times I truly felt I was losing my mind. The struggle to become and over comer has not been easy. There were times when I thought about just giving up. I was very revengeful, bitter, sad, mad, ashamed, confused, betrayed and I even felt hopeless. Scripture tells us hope deferred makes a heart sick. I was truly sick in heart. So many things in my life are different now. In fact, my whole life had changed. I tried drinking alcohol, smoking marijuana, and smoking tons of cigarettes. I thought that all of these things would help dull the pain. I wanted to escape it all. I was so wrong! Instead, I seemed to be sinking, just drowning in sorrow and pain. This combination of habits would lead me down a path to disaster. When the alcohol made me sick, I would still try to drink. The Holy Spirit got my attention and as a result, I knew God was not pleased with the things I began doing. Those things were unhealthy and unsafe. When everything wore off, I felt even more depressed and frustrated. There was nowhere to run and nowhere to hide to get away from what had happened to me that one night. This was certainly not a dream. Nothing seemed to be working for me. I got back on my knees and prayed to the Lord to help me find myself again. I prayed, *Lord, help me to love myself again. Fix my life. Take away this hate in my heart and grant me happiness.* I wanted Him to help me accept what I couldn't change and let me be more thankful for a second chance at life. I sincerely knew in my heart that I had not forgiven Jamar. So, I prayed to God to help me forgive myself because the forgiveness was for me and not Jamar. In my heart, I believed if I just let go of the hate and turn it over to God, I would receive the healing I so desperately needed. I had faith and I believed that God could and would fix my life.

I was in a different place with Wesley. I had gotten to that place through prayer and getting in a quiet place. God had told me it was time to move on. I understood what letting Wesley go meant. I had to let go to get my transformation. Man did not complete me, God did. Once I let him go I was able to completely surrender to God. It took two years to completely let Wesley go. I was still holding on. I would hear the Holy Spirit minister to me and tell me, "You need to let God lead and guide you. Let go. This is not the life that God wants for you." The Holy Spirit was steadily telling me to let him go. *What am I going to do then?* I would ask within myself and the Holy Spirit told me that I was going to keep living. The best is yet to come. I had to trust in God and have faith.

The last time the Holy Spirit told me it was time, I said, "Alright. I'll listen." It was Thanksgiving and I called him and told him how thankful I was to have him in my life but I no longer wanted to be in relationship with him as we were. If we were going to get married, it must be now or never, and we weren't, and I truly wanted more for my life. I felt like Wesley was in a good place for himself but that was not a good enough place for me—especially not with the Holy Spirit on my case to leave him alone.

God was letting me out of the relationship with Wesley. I stopped dating and I stopped drinking. I didn't get high anymore and it is still a struggle to not smoke a cigarette. Amazingly as soon as I was able to completely let go great things started happening. I was at peace with myself. I wasn't afraid to be alone by myself. God fixed it so that I realized I was never by myself and I wouldn't be.

I smoking marijuana and stayed in church. I was able to hide my vocal cord damage and still sing solos. I got new friends who were saved and who loved serving the Lord. As God blessed me to face reality, I began to move forward. I realized I didn't need someone to complete me, God had—and has—everything I needed. I completely committed myself to serving God and talking with women who were abused. I stopped dating and riding the motorcycle. My life started looking up and getting better slowly but surely. My friends now are Christians who love the Lord. I am blessed to have friends who are like family and are very loving and supportive.

Working in church has been and is a great accomplishment in my life. Now that I'm helping others I now have no time to feel sorry for myself. I want to be able to be a blessing with my testimony. I needed so badly to help someone. I do not want any other person to suffer mentally or physically the way that I did. I was determined to be a difference maker. However, I had to get myself where I needed to be. It all starts with you. I asked God for strength and He did just what I asked. I would meet once a week with a group of women at church. I would advise them where they could get help and counseling. I even counseled some ladies myself. Why shouldn't I? I had been there and had gone through worst things just through that one time. I felt needed! I was really getting myself together. One young lady who I ministered to wouldn't listen to counseling and was killed at twenty-three years old.

Yes, I still had my own fears but definitely not like it had been in the past. The bitterness left and all I wanted to do was live and not kill myself anymore. God truly brought me back to reality. He took me through a transformation. I started feeling like the old Jane again. There's nothing I can do that can erase what has happened to me. I know I will never forget.

After my transformation back to reality and back to knowing I could do anything with God being the head of my life, God blessed me with a loving husband: Manno. Together we make a great team! Both of us are working in the church and sincere in reaching souls.

Today, I still thank God for that part of my life. Many of the riders have since gone on to Glory. They all played a very instrumental part in my healing. I will never ever forget them. God knows who you need and when you need them in your life. Trust God and He will do it every time. After what seemed like seven years of riding on motorcycles, I found the path that God would have me to be on now and that is ministry to the abused.

During a session with women who were involved in domestic abuse, there was a female who was afraid to get out of her vehicle to enter her apartment. She worked at night and lived on a dead end street near a wooded area. Her estranged husband on several occasions would be waiting for her as she opened her door. She lived in constant fear and stated she was not getting the help she needed from the police. When asked what I could advise her with other than prayer, I suggested a gun. She had been badly beaten on several occasions by the husband. I felt it was to her advantage to use common sense to protect herself.

My pastor at the time, was very much against weapons. But this was about using common sense. I felt it would be to her advantage to be able to protect herself. I too used common sense in having a way to protect myself.

Another woman I met had been in an abusive relationship for years and had been cut off from her family by her husband. Her family thought that she was in a happy relationship and doing well. She covered up what her husband had done and what was going on in her life with the beatings. She attended no family gatherings. Her reason for staying with her husband was she didn't think that she could make it by herself. She didn't work and she had small children. If his food wasn't seasoned right he would beat her. If she didn't answer the phone in an appropriate number of rings, he would beat her. He would make her clean the floors with a brush. He constantly accused her of looking at other men. When he went out drinking, she had to live a life of pure hell. Not only did he beat her but he would force sex on her. She would take up for him and say he was not like that all the time. She felt she had done something to set him off. He would say he was sorry and that he would not hit her again. However, this continued for several months after I had met her. Of course we would always pray. She finally got the nerves to get away from her abuser. She relocated and is remarried. I don't know where she is today but I pray that all is well.

I remember a lady saying, "I've called the police several times. I'm not getting the help I need. My boyfriend calls on the phone to entice my son to let him in when II am at work. I'm terrified. What would you do if this was you?" My answer was, "Buy a gun because you have the God-given right to protect you and your child. If you shoot him, make sure he's dead." That may not have been the absolute best advice but it was the truth. She bought a gun, learned how to shoot it, and has since relocated to Texas. Her boyfriend is in jail for second-degree murder of someone else.

My minister and I were not in agreement with my advising an abused female to buy a weapon but I'd heard from the Holy Spirit and this particular victim needed to use common sense. In all honesty she couldn't just sit and wait for someone who'd threatened her and her child to do bodily harm or possibly kill her. This lady had been beaten several times by him.

Women found out about my abuse ministry after hearing my testimony during Sunday's worship at church.

The secretary announced women would meet the third Friday of each month at 6pm. Women attending church services were told to invite someone they knew who was being abused and to also invite young women of dating age to attend. This would help them to know what abuse is. The first meeting consisted of fifteen ladies of different ages and races. This ministry took ten years to become full blown.

Praying for someone else is what I needed to do. My minister at the time of my road to recovery heard my testimony one Sunday and prophesied to me that God had said my ministry would be to help abused women. I had already heard from God. My minister's prophesy was just a confirmation of what God had already spoken. So I started meeting and working with women through my church. Some were members and others were invited by members. God allowed me to feel women who were around me that were in pain through hugs, smiles and just saying to them that God loves them and I love them, too. I'd reassure them that whatever they were going through, God could certainly bring them out.

After meeting with groups of women and sharing my testimony, they opened up and began to trust me. Several women were delivered from violent domestic situations. Women were slain in the spirit through this fellowship. Healing took place!

When I encountered a female who was hurting from abuse, I would pray with her and chills would run through my body. I could actually feel this person's pain. These meetings also included young women who were being controlled by boyfriends. It helped them to open their eyes to what could happen after being yelled at, cursed, and pushed around which showed they were not being treated like a lady. For many of them, I had to give them straight talk and tell them "if you stay, you will die" or "If you won't straighten up for yourself, straighten up for your family." God saw fit that when they were ready for help, I was prepared to help them.

RECOVERING DAILY

TODAY I HAVE NO IDEA WHERE MY ABUSER IS. However, I pray on a daily basis for God to cover me! I pray for God to dispatch His angels to keep me from any hurt, harm or danger. Yes, I'm still alert, looking everywhere I go. I make it a habit to let someone know where I'm at all times. I have a great support system. For 24 years, I have been blessed with my new friends that love me and care for me. I'm grateful for my friends who helped me to build up my self esteem, and those that prayed with me and for me.

My mother aged quickly after my abuse. Her health declined rapidly seeing her baby girl suffer and her not being able to fix it. It really took a toll on her life. She is currently 82 years of age in a nursing home due to a blood clot on the brain and Alzheimer's and not aware of her existence. The doctors said she might have had Alzheimer's ten or fifteen years before I knew it. But I can recall her mind going down during the time she took care of me. I visit her often and pray with and for her. I know my mother's love for me is truly a blessing from God. She told me I would always be her little princess and she will always love me as I will always love her. I thank God that before she lost her eye sight, she was able to see the fixed me. She expressed her joy and happiness of my new found life and blessings. She knew she didn't have to worry about me being hurt anymore because I have a wonderful husband that she adores. She called him her son, one of the apples of her eyes. So you see, you too can make it through. You must however pray and keep the faith. God can fix anything and anyone. He fixed my heart and my body. All praise and glory belongs to The Lord! Never give up your chance to be free. God truly has the final say so!

Look at just how He made a way for me. He brought light to the very dark areas of my life, and when I thought of giving up on life the Holy Ghost told me to hold on to God's unchanging hands. God is still taking me through as I can only take things one day at a time. My life is a living testimony and I owe it all to God. God is truly the head of my life! It only happened to me one time and the abuse almost cost me my life. But glory be to God I made it and I'm an overcomer. You can be an overcomer, too!

Even through pain and suffering, God will supply your every need. But you must have faith and trust that God will give you the strength to overcome. Don't spend the rest of your life trying to get even with your abuser. The battle is not yours, it's the Lord's! I bet some of you have tried every way that you know how to get even with your abuser. But let me recommend Jesus! With Jesus you will get the blueprint needed to become an overcomer. So reach up and pull down your blessings. God is just waiting for you to call upon Him for help. Make no mistake you can live a productive life. Therefore, you must be precise and specific when calling on the Name of Jesus. You must believe, believe, and believe that God loves us all the same. As I sit here writing this book, it takes me back to things I'll always remember like the time when my mouth was wired and having to communicate on paper because I just couldn't talk. How we take a little thing for granted. Our walk, our talk we take these and more for granted. I'm reminded of vocal cord damage from being severely choked. I experience sore throat and ear aches from ruptured ear drums and a collapsed lung. I'll always have respiratory problems. There are times when I have trouble breathing. Thank God I have a machine to take breathing treatments. I daily use inhalers. In spite of all the things I have to live with because of the forced trauma in my life I still give God all the praise for a second chance at life. My life is happy now! I'm alive and free from abuse!

You see God can give you peace, joy, happiness and unconditional love. God's grace and mercies are the reasons why I'm here today to tell the whole world what happened to me. I pray that this will be an encouragement to someone who's hurting. Always remember, if there are children involved they will hurt too. They will need help also.

Stop feeling guilty and sorry for yourself. Give your life to God right this minute. Get in a word church where the uncompromised word of God is being taught and preached. You cannot do this alone. This is not your fault. No matter what is happening or has happened you don't deserve to be abused. Your life is worth so much more. You have the right to have a happy life. Your children deserve to be in a stable loving secure household. Reach out to your local support groups. There is help for you. The first step is admitting you need and want help so you can have happiness in your life. God is love! If you have been hit or cursed at take precautions. Abuse of any kind is wrong. You don't want to be a statistic.

When you receive your healing from God, be sure to reach out and help someone else. This will definitely help you heal more. You may never forget but with God you can go on to live that productive life. Because of what happened to me, I've made domestic violence my business. This is my ministry! I declare as long as I live, I will do whatever I can to help some woman or man look to God for the strength they need. God can be whatever you need Him to be! I call upon The Lord anytime of the day or night and I am a living witness that God hears and answers prayers.

As I sit here, 24 years after the attack, doctor's visits are still frequent. My doctor has asked me to consider throat surgery and surgery to help close the hole behind my septum. They think it would aid in my swallowing. But, I've just had enough of the surgeries now, and I don't want them to use animal skin to attempt to close the hole behind my septum. I lose air at night and stop breathing because of the septum. I've developed asthma and the doctors say that it is also related to the attack. No feeling in the right side of my face, only last year—2013—have I been able to feel the cold from ice in my mouth.

There are times when I've gone into depression. I wanted no food, no clothes on, no doctor's appointment. I just lay and talk to the Lord and He pulls me out of it. I don't take the medicines for depression because they control me and make me hallucinate. My husband is my guardian angel. He can feel that something is wrong with me. His relationship with God allows him to know I'm going through something. I remember when he wouldn't sleep and would watch me sleep. I'm glad he sleeps now. I am noticing that my face is again starting to droop. Age and elasticity is setting in but I will not let them go back in and add bones.

Whatever happens at this point, I can live with it. It does not weigh on me now as much as it use to how people look at me or what they think. My thing now is, God loves me and I really don't care what anybody else thinks. Don't get me wrong I do have those moments. Once you've been abused, you never forget. I allow people to see what I want them to see and what I don't want them to see I can hide it. I've learned how to cover it up.

I've tried to shelter and push this away.

This was so painful. I didn't want to think about it, and I've placed it deep within my memory and wanted it forgotten. I wanted the circle of abuse to be cut off from my mind.

As I reflect back on this, I can see where on that one day of abuse, that one day of beating, God was trying to save me. Had I had the relationship with God that I have now, where I am sensitive to His character and voice, I would have saw the jammed door as a sign and would have slowed down just a second and said, "God what's this about?" and I believe He would have allowed me to sense the danger. I am so grateful that I have that relationship now with God and I encourage everyone I meet to yield their hearts toward God. It is the difference between life and death.

THE FIXED ME

IS THERE ANYTHING TOO HARD FOR GOD? I SAY not! God is able to do exceedingly, abundantly above all we can think or imagine according to the holy anointed power that's in us. Thank God for the wisdom and the knowledge imparted to the physicians. Hospital stays were not easy. But God!

The Fixed Me details how the great physicians put me back together again.

I did not have the relationship with God I have now and I didn't know when the Holy Spirit was warning me. As I look back if I had the relationship with God that I have now I never would have had the incident happen. But that's not all we need in life sometimes. A lot of times what we see is the devil in sheep's clothing when we don't have the connection with God.

God already knew what was going to happen to me. I don't have an answer why. I wonder where my life would be. Everything that happens happens for a reason. My reason could have really been that God ordained me to help someone else. There are so many forms of abuse but they are all different. Before this happened to me I had God in my life but not the way I needed to. I could have still been lost out there if this had not happened to me. It's like God was saying, "Jane, you are too valuable. I need you to stay here."

The attack drew me to my destiny. This book is my destiny. Touching your life as you read this is my destiny. God left me here to touch you. When I realized God gave me a second chance a life to hear the birds, feel the sun, and see the rain, all of that meant so much to me. After that happened to me, everything became beautiful to me.

But I hold on to God's unchanging hand. I continue to pray and claim my healings. I won't complain! Everyday has been and continues to be an adventure for me but I'm determined to enjoy life and be grateful for God giving me a second chance at life. Each and every morning when God opens my eyes to behold a brand new day, I give Him thanks and praise because I'm still here. I'm alive! I'm happy in spite of the illnesses. There's nothing impossible for God!

I've learned to definitely walk by faith and not by sight! I've been blessed to have faith that believes the impossible and be that living witness to see the impossible being extended on my behalf. God had me! God carried me! I thank God that the surgeons had the wisdom and knowledge to know what to do and when to do it. I thank God!

One hundred and eighty-seven clamps to close up my face. More than two hundred clamps to close up my head. There are screws in the bones in my mouth to hold my teeth in and a plate in the top of my mouth to help with talking. A right eye that's been re-socket and rebuilt so it can close like the other. A fixed septum with the flimsy skin that surrounded my brain. In addition the usage of the fine bone in my head to rebuild the right side of my face, my tongue fixed so it would move as it should and the doctors made me another nose.

The Fixed Me!

I have no feelings on the right side of my face. I lose air when I'm asleep but I'm still alive! I came out of this and I thank God!

Even now, I don't care for hospitals. I dread doctor's appointments. After having twenty-seven surgeries for reconstruction purposes and a life time of thirty-one surgeries it's no wonder. I've had so many stinking infections. The inside of my head was irrigated before the plates in it could be removed. As a result, I was nauseous from smelling infections. But it was in me and it stunk. No one could imagine the mental anguish, the suffering, the constant nightmares, the shamefulness of how I looked, the feeling of helplessness being without an eye. It was a rough walk. But I knew I wasn't in this by myself. My God was with me all the time. The many surgeries have truly been a blessing. They helped to make The Fixed Me.

I couldn't give up! I couldn't quit! I kept demanding God's help. I kept listening to His instructions. God didn't give up! He took me through it and I'm mighty, mighty grateful. He alone gave me the strength! I thank God! The Fixed Me is with a right eye that when I'm asleep it doesn't close because of the damage to the muscles and tissues. When I blow my nose it comes out of my nose but also out of the corner of my right eye. If my eye is irritated or infected it affects my sinuses. If I have problems with my sinuses my right eye cries. But I'm here! To God be all the glory! I sleep on a lot of pillows due to breathing problems. I must have cold air at all times. The improper breathing comes from the hole behind the septum. I take more than twelve medications per day.

In 1999, while dating Manno, my daughter abandoned her children. The state was going to put my three grandsons in foster care. My doctor advised me not to take the boys. However, I prayed and went against the physician's advice. I couldn't bear them not being around family and to be separated and know that there would be a possibility that they would get lost in the system. They needed me and my love and they were hurting and afraid. I too needed to be love and wanted. The children needed special love and care, stability, security, understanding and much patience. So I stepped out on faith. My family members helped with them for one school term. After which I moved them into my home. My new husband really supported me. He loved me enough to be the Christian father figure that my grandsons needed in their lives. The children had therapy because of abuse of various nature. We kept them grounded and rooted in church. We let them know that we loved them and would always be there for them. God blessed me to be able to do for the kids and give them what they needed in their lives. Sadly, we have not seen my daughter in fourteen years.

We were blessed to get two out of the three boys out of high school. Two have since moved out on their own but still dealing with the repercussion of having been abused. However, the 26-year-old may never move. He is working and not a bit of a problem. I thank the Lord that He spared my life because my grandkids needed me, and I'm grateful that even though it wasn't easy due to ongoing medical problems, my heart was big enough to be there for them. You see God already knew what would happen and He made a way for me to do what was needed to help hurting and confused children. Thank you, Lord, for all You have done in my life because it just keep on getting better as the days go by.

In spite of it all, I know God to be my all and all. I know Him to be Jehovah Jireh, My Provider. I know Him to be Jehovah Shalom, my peace; Jehovah Rapha, my healer; Jehovah Rohi, my shepherd; Jehovah-Nissi, my banner; and Jehovah-Shammah, The Lord is there. He was there all along. He had the angels watching over me. He was there! Because of God Almighty, I'm a better person. I'm stronger, wiser, and put no one above Him. He restored my soul. He's elevated my faith system. That measure of faith I had in the beginning has multiplied. With God as your captain you'll never go wrong or be alone. We are blessed!

I thank God for a second chance at life. It is an awesome feeling to be delivered from your darkest hours, and see God's marvelous light. It is a miracle from God that I have been allowed to have a happy life. All my faith and trust is in God. My sisters and brothers God never fails. Anything you need God has it. From the bottom of my heart I thank God that I am still alive. Remember this abuse happened one time and one time should be enough for anyone. Okay you've read what happened to me only one time and as a result I almost lost my life. It is my prayer that someone who reads about my journey from domestic abuse will be delivered. It is our God given right to be in a loving, safe secured relationship. God is about love and each and every one of us deserves to be loved. I've shared my testimony to be a blessing to those of you who are hurting because of abuse. I sincerely pray that you be delivered from the pain of violation to the mind and to the body.

I pray that no other man or woman will ever have to endure the pain I have gone through. I pray that someone reading this book will open their eyes and see what happened to me or worse than what happened to me could happen to them. It is time for you to reach out and open your mouth and speak up to get the help you need and the help your children need. Remember you can be an overcomer. You can live a happy and prosperous life. Stop letting anyone beat on you. Let go of the shame and remember abuse is not your fault. Stop making excuses and covering up for your abuser. Speak to your local church groups and other support groups that are available so you can get help and be safe. Don't allow your abuser to keep you from having the life you deserve. Open your heart to God and let God in. Give God your life and let God lead and guide you. Through a personal relationship with God you will come out from the darkness into God's marvelous light. Have faith in God! The abuse you've suffered follows you through life. However, through prayer we do learn to live with what has happened to us and go on with a productive life. Keep praying because it does get better. Keep God at the head of your life and spend time talking to God and giving Him praise on a daily basis. You have my word God will take you through all the stuff you've endured. You can make it! I made it! Now domestic abuse is my business! I can truly say I've been delivered and set free. I am healed and I thank God I'm an overcomer.

I lost Quinton as a teen and I am daily working to restore my son as an adult currently incarcerated in Louisiana State Penitentiary in Angola. But I know he can't be an overcomer until he gives his anger, the desire for revenge, and his life to God. It's never too late to ask God for forgiveness and do what's right. God is a God of many chances and is always on time. He never leaves or forsakes you. God is always available. Yes, Manno and I did everything we could to help my son get a new start in life. He didn't want a regular job. He wanted the quick money that leads to trouble. He told my new husband, thanks man for loving my mom and taking care of her the way you do. She smiles again because you are good to her. I don't have to worry about her being hurt anymore and I thank you sir. I still miss my child. He's a 39-year-old man now. Most of his life, he's been locked up. Yes, Manno and I are here for Quinton. We desired to give him love, to guide him spiritually, emotionally, mentally and financially. We did everything in our power and with prayer to be there for him. He still says he doesn't worry about me anymore and he loves my husband for loving me with respect.

Quinton has never wanted me to see him "locked up like a mad man," he said. I miss him so much, but I know God's taking care of him. If he wasn't locked up he would probably be dead right now. I will continue to reach out to help my son in any way I can. I'll keep speaking this to him until he receives it in his heart, mind, body and soul.

God is the answer! He must get past the hate, anger, and bitterness and until he does he'll continue on a path of destruction.

If I didn't have God in my life where in the world would I be today? After this happened to me I could only think about survival. What can I do to fix me up to take the eyes off of me? God would have to direct the doctors' hands and minds on what to do. I knew then that there has got to be a reason for this. I'm a happy 61-year-old now and God has blessed me with a wonderful spouse. We've been happily married for thirteen years and he loves me unconditionally. He prays for me and he prays with me. I still have some illnesses as a result of the attack. This year I have been sick a lot but with the Lord as my head and Manno by my side, I can't help but be a survivor.

MY CHARGE TO YOU

MY CHARGE TO YOU IS TO TELL SOMEONE WHAT you are going through. You have no reason to be ashamed. (If you are not being abused but you fear that someone you love is being abused. I charge you to go into an earnest prayer for them and share this book with them.) You have no reason to be ashamed. There are so many resources available to help you live a protected life. Don't be afraid to develop a safety plan and go on with your life. Don't be afraid to leave now with your children and run to safety. A lot of victims of domestic violence don't live to tell what happened to them. Even though, it only happened once, my abuse has affected every day of my life, of my children's lives, of my mother's life, and even my husband's life. You deserve help. You deserve freedom.

Abuse is wrong even if it happened only one time. It is wrong for women and wrong for men. No one deserves to be abused. After almost losing my life at the hand of a man, I've made abuse my business. It's a personal issue. I've had to relive a devastating time in my life to be able to write this book, but for this book to be able to help someone, then it will be a rewarded blessing in my life.

My charge to you is to make sure you have a personal relationship with God so the Holy Spirit can speak to you, lead, and guide you. Seek God for your mate in life. Be specific about your requests. Wait on God. Don't be hasty. Don't be vulnerable. Make sure you hear from God. God doesn't make mistakes. Understand that if a man or woman doesn't love the Lord, then they can't possibly love you and can't treat you the way God has ordained for you to be treated, loved, and cherished. Love does not hurt.

There is love, hope, joy, peace, and happiness in our lives when we truly love the Lord and have a relationship with him. Trust God and see won't He provide everything you need. God is your security blanket. You can call upon him for anything and at anytime. He is never too busy for His children. Know that you have a right to not be abused and no matter what you have done, you don't deserve to be abused.

Not sure if your situation is abuse? Ask yourself these questions:

- Does your mate call you stupid, ugly, and says nobody wants you?

- Does your mate make you do things over and over to their satisfaction and berates you like a child?

- Do you lie for your mate?

- Has your mate hit you, shoved you or cursed you?

- Do you have a constant feeling that something is wrong with your mate and they may quickly over react?

- Does your mate pick fights with you so they can have an excuse to go party and stay out all night?

- Does your mate isolate you from family and friends?

- Does your mate accuse you of having other relationships? (Even going as far as checking your under clothes or private parts for signs of sexual activity.)

- Do you stay with your mate for fear of what will happen if you leave?

If your answer is yes, you should call the National Domestic Abuse hotline at 800-799-7233 from a private or secure telephone.

www.ingramcontent.com/pod-product-compliance
Lightning Source LLC
Chambersburg PA
CBHW071143090426
42736CB00012B/2207